BIGGEST NAMES IN SPORTS

# NIKOLA JOKIĆ

## BASKETBALL STAR

by Harold P. Cain



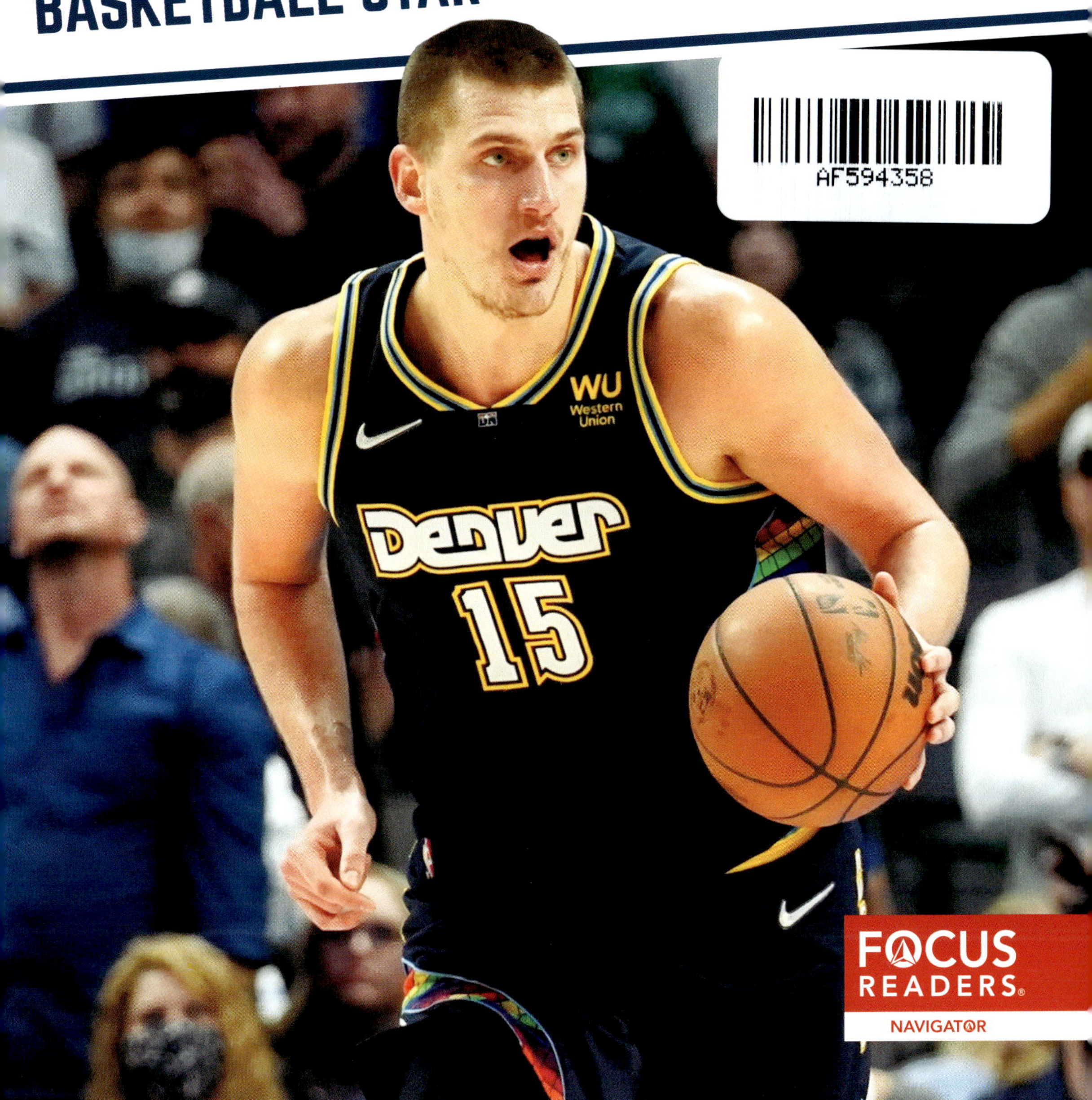


FOCUS READERS®
NAVIGATOR

WWW.FOCUSREADERS.COM



Focus Readers is distributed by North Star Editions:
sales@northstareditions.com | 888-417-0195

Produced for Focus Readers by Red Line Editorial.

Photographs ©: Tony Gutierrez/AP Images, cover, 1; Jim Mone/AP Images, 4–5; Tom Lynn/AP Images, 7; David Zalubowski/AP Images, 9, 21; Shutterstock Images, 10–11; Roman Vondrous/CTK/AP Images, 13; Jack Dempsey/AP Images, 15; Hector Acevedo/Cal Sport Media/AP Images, 16–17; Darren Abate/AP Images, 19; Eric Gay/AP Images, 22–23; Mark J. Terrill/AP Images, 25; Adam Hunger/AP Images, 27; Red Line Editorial, 29

**Library of Congress Cataloging-in-Publication Data**
Library of Congress Cataloging-in-Publication Data is available on the Library of Congress website.

**ISBN**
978-1-63739-257-7 (hardcover)
978-1-63739-309-3 (paperback)
978-1-63739-410-6 (ebook pdf)
978-1-63739-361-1 (hosted ebook)

Printed in the United States of America
Mankato, MN
082022

## ABOUT THE AUTHOR

Harold P. Cain is a retired English teacher and lifelong sports fan originally from Rockford, Illinois. He and his wife now live in Cathedral City, California, where they enjoy hiking, golf, and spending time with their daughter and three grandchildren in Los Angeles.

# TABLE OF CONTENTS

WU
WESTERN
UNION
DENVER
15
SPALDING

CHAPTER 1

# RACING TO HISTORY

Nikola Jokić received a pass near the baseline. The Denver Nuggets center bullied his way to the hoop and put up a shot. Giannis Antetokounmpo, the towering Milwaukee Bucks forward, blocked it. But Jokić didn't quit. He grabbed the **rebound** and laid it back in for two.

**Nikola Jokić averaged 18.5 points per game during the 2017–18 season.**

There wasn't anything special about the game on February 15, 2018. Jokić said he wasn't more motivated than usual. But he sure played like he was.

On the next Bucks possession, Jokić stole the ball. He made a perfect pass to teammate Will Barton, who nailed a three-pointer. A minute later, Jokić blocked a shot from Khris Middleton. Then he sent a long pass that set up another Nuggets three.

Midway through the second quarter, Jokić showed his own shooting range. Most players his size stay close to the basket. But Jokić isn't most players. He caught a pass at the top of the

Jokić attempts to block a shot by Milwaukee Bucks forward Tony Snell.

three-point line. Then he released a shot that hit nothing but net.

The numbers were piling up for Jokić. He soon went over 10 points. He got his 10th rebound a few minutes later. These stats weren't new for Jokić. In his third season, he was used to putting up big numbers. But he didn't usually get them so quickly.

Time was running out in the half. With just under two minutes to go, Jokić held the ball. He spotted teammate Wilson Chandler behind the three-point line. Jokić hit him with a pass, and Chandler drained the shot. That was Jokić's 10th assist of the night. He had achieved a **triple-double**.

It was the fastest triple-double in the history of the National Basketball Association (NBA). Jokić did it in just 14 minutes and 33 seconds of playing time. He beat the old record by more than two minutes.

Jokić recorded 10 triple-doubles in the 2017–18 season.

Jokić finished the game with 30 points, 15 rebounds, and 17 assists. Only five other players had achieved all those totals in a game. Four of them were Hall of Famers. Only time would tell if Jokić would join them.

# CHAPTER 2

# SERBIAN STAR

Nikola Jokić was born on February 19, 1995. He grew up in the small town of Sombor, Serbia. Nikola loved basketball. However, it wasn't easy to watch NBA games in Serbia. He had to settle for watching old highlights of Michael Jordan or Kobe Bryant.

**Sombor, Serbia, is home to approximately 50,000 people.**

Pro teams in Serbia began to notice Nikola. In 2012, at age 17, he signed his first pro **contract**. Nikola joined Mega Vizura, a team in Serbia's capital city of Belgrade. Nikola played mostly on the junior team at first. But by 2013–14, he started to earn more playing time on the senior team.

## FAMILY BUSINESS

**Both of Nikola's older brothers also played basketball. His brother Strahinja had a long pro career in Serbia. His brother Nemanja played college basketball in the United States. Besides his brothers, Nikola had another basketball influence in NBA player Darko Miličić. The Serbian native was friends with Nikola's brothers growing up.**

Jokić (7) competes in the 2013 FIBA U19 World Championship.

Though he was still a teenager, Nikola stood 6 feet 11 inches (211 cm) tall. He weighed 252 pounds (114 kg). That size and strength helped him on the court. But Nikola wasn't just big. He was also a good shooter and passer. In 2013–14, Nikola averaged 11.4 points and 6.4 rebounds per game. And he did it against pro players who were much older.

Nikola dreamed of playing in the NBA. In 2014, he was eligible for the **draft**. However, he wasn't sure any team would draft him. Nikola was still young. He wouldn't be ready to play in the NBA right away. Even so, the Denver Nuggets took a chance on his potential. They chose him 41st overall. Nikola was asleep when it happened. His brother Nemanja called him with the good news.

The next year, Nikola took on a main role with Mega Vizura. He averaged 15.4 points per game. He also led the league with 9.3 rebounds per game. That

Jokić poses for a photo after signing with the Denver Nuggets in 2015.

helped him win the Adriatic League's Most Valuable Player (MVP) Award. It also showed he was ready for the next level. Nikola announced he would join the Nuggets that summer. The kid from Serbia was going to the NBA.

SPALDING
15

CHAPTER 3

# WELCOME TO THE NBA

Nikola Jokić had shown that he had **elite** basketball skills. But he still had plenty of work to do. That included changing his diet. Jokić used to drink a gallon of soda every day. When the Nuggets drafted him, he promised to eat healthier.

**Jokić throws down a dunk during his rookie season.**

Expectations were low for Jokić in his **rookie** season. Few fans had even heard of him. Jokić mostly came off the bench. However, he shined when given the chance to play.

Jokić had a **breakout** game in November 2015. Facing the San Antonio Spurs, he showed his soft touch around the rim with 23 points. He also grabbed 12 rebounds. Jokić started to earn more playing time. And he made the most of those minutes. Jokić finished the season third in Rookie of the Year voting.

By his second season, Jokić had become the go-to offensive option for the Nuggets. In one game, Jokić racked up

Jokić battles for a rebound against the San Antonio Spurs during a 2015 game.

20 points, 12 rebounds, and 11 assists in a win over the Milwaukee Bucks. It marked his first triple-double. A week later, Jokić scored a career-high 40 points in a win against the New York Knicks.

Jokić was even better in 2017–18. He developed into an elite passer and shooter. Those are skills common in guards and forwards. But Jokić was doing it as a center. That season, he averaged a double-double of 18.5 points and 10.7 rebounds per game.

Jokić helped the Nuggets finish with a record of 46–36. It was the team's first

## NATIONAL PRIDE

**In 2016, Jokić played for Serbia at the Olympic Games in Brazil. He led his team in rebounding and helped Serbia reach the gold-medal game. However, they settled for silver after losing 96–66 to Team USA.**

Jokić muscles his way toward the basket against Wesley Matthews of the Dallas Mavericks in 2018.

winning season in five years. Jokić's record-setting triple-double against the Bucks came in February of this season. As Jokić improved, so did the Nuggets.

GAY
22
MILE HIGH
15
CITY
10

# CHAPTER 4

# BREAKING OUT

In 2018–19, Nikola Jokić made his first All-Star Game. The Nuggets won 54 games that season. They also reached the **playoffs** for the first time in six years. That gave Jokić a new stage to shine on.

The opening series against the Spurs was tight. Jokić scored 43 points in a Game 6 loss. In Game 7, Jokić posted a

Jokić puts up a shot during a 2019 playoff game against the Spurs.

triple-double to send the Nuggets to the next round. Unfortunately for Nuggets fans, Denver lost to the Portland Trail Blazers. But Jokić proved he could play against the NBA's top teams.

Jokić's best moments of 2019–20 came in the playoffs. In the first round, Denver trailed the Utah Jazz three games to one. But the Nuggets battled back. In Game 7, Jokić sank a game-winning hook shot.

In the next round, Denver faced the Los Angeles Clippers. Once again, the Nuggets went down three games to one. And once again, the Nuggets fought their way back. In Game 7, Jokić recorded a triple-double and helped Denver come

Jokić attempts a shot against the Los Angeles Clippers during the 2020 playoffs.

out on top. Denver fell to the eventual NBA champions, the Los Angeles Lakers, in the next round. But there was no doubting Jokić's ability.

In 2020–21, Jokić put together his best season yet. He averaged 26.4 points, 10.8 rebounds, and 8.3 assists per game. Those were all the best numbers of his career. And it earned him the NBA MVP Award. Jokić was the lowest-drafted player ever to win it.

## THE SOMBOR SHUFFLE

Jokić injured his left ankle in 2017. As a result, he began shooting off his right foot. He became so good that he developed a signature shot. He starts by leaning in with his left foot. Then he shoots the ball off his right foot while fading away from the basket. The shot is nicknamed "The Sombor Shuffle."

Jokić drives toward the basket during a 2022 game against the Brooklyn Nets.

Jokić didn't slow down in 2021–22. In December, he recorded his 60th career triple-double. With that, he passed Hall of Famer Larry Bird for eighth all time. Jokić was already in the company of legends.

# NIKOLA JOKIĆ

- Height: 6 feet 11 inches (211 cm)
- Weight: 284 pounds (129 kg)
- Birth date: February 19, 1995
- Birthplace: Sombor, Serbia
- European teams: Mega Vizura (Belgrade, Serbia) (2012–15)
- NBA team: Denver Nuggets (2015–)
- Major awards: Olympic silver medal (2016); NBA All-Star (2019–21); NBA MVP (2021)

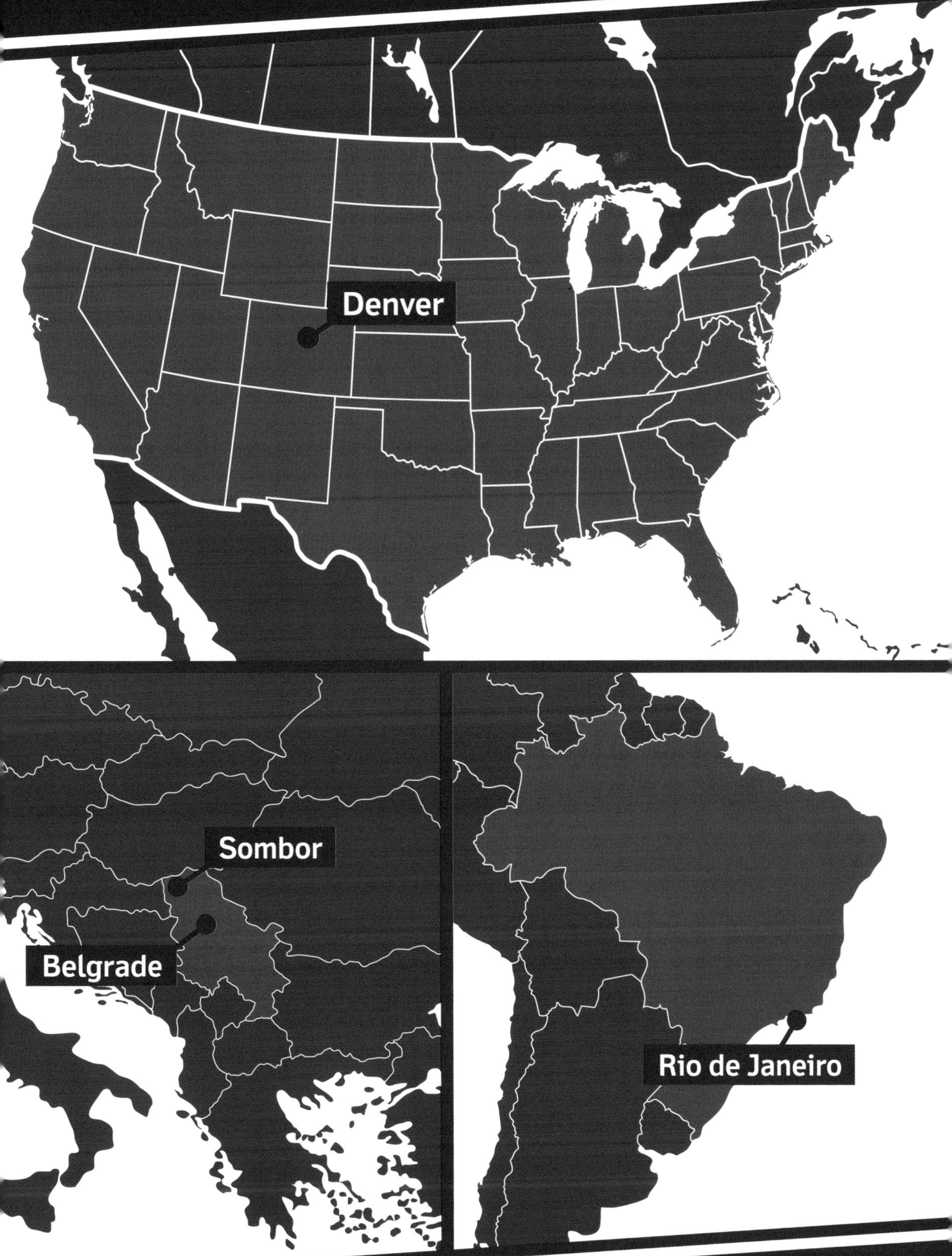
Denver
Sombor
Belgrade
Rio de Janeiro

## FOCUS ON
# NIKOLA JOKIĆ

*Write your answers on a separate piece of paper.*

**1.** Write a sentence that describes the main idea of Chapter 2.

**2.** Which of Jokić's skills do you think is most important? Why?

**3.** What was Jokić doing when he was drafted by the Nuggets in 2014?

  **A.** sleeping
  **B.** eating
  **C.** playing basketball

**4.** Why are triple-doubles an important basketball statistic?

  **A.** They show that someone is only good at shooting.
  **B.** They show that someone is a good all-around player.
  **C.** They show that someone is not good at rebounding.

*Answer key on page 32.*

# GLOSSARY

**breakout**
Having to do with a sudden success.

**contract**
An agreement to pay someone a certain amount of money.

**draft**
A system that allows teams to acquire new players coming into a league.

**elite**
The best of the best.

**playoffs**
A set of games played after the regular season to decide which team will be the champion.

**rebound**
A play in which a player controls the ball after a missed shot.

**rookie**
A professional athlete in his or her first year.

**triple-double**
A game in which a player has double-digit numbers in three categories. The categories are often points, assists, and rebounds.

# TO LEARN MORE

## BOOKS


Flynn, Brendan. *The NBA Encyclopedia for Kids*. Minneapolis: Abdo Publishing, 2022.

Mahoney, Brian. *GOATs of Basketball*. Minneapolis: Abdo Publishing, 2022.

Savage, Jeff. *Basketball Super Stats*. Minneapolis: Lerner Publications, 2018.


## NOTE TO EDUCATORS

Visit **www.focusreaders.com** to find lesson plans, activities, links, and other resources related to this title.

# INDEX



**Answer Key: 1.** Answers will vary; **2.** Answers will vary; **3.** A; **4.** B